Jan to Tamarind

poems about the color brown

Poems by
Malathi Michelle Iyengar

Illustrations by
Jamel Akib

Children's Book Press · San Francisco, California

Tan

Brown.
  Milk-tea brown.
    Spicy-sweet *masala* tea brown.

Tea leaves and cardamom,
ginger and clove.

Amma steeps them in hot-hot water,
adds lots of cream and sugar.

Sweet, milky brown.
Delicate, fragrant brown.

My milk-tea brown hands
  hold a cup of spicy tan *masala* tea,
    to sip on a golden-brown summer afternoon.

Sienna

Brown.
Sienna brown.
Rusty, dusty, coppery brown.

Reddish-brown mountains,
our Southwest home.

Dad hears coyotes calling,
I spot their sandy tracks.

Four o'clock breeze
drifts the smell of sage
across our sienna path.

Strong, unyielding brown.
Warm, abiding brown.

Keep going! You can make it!
We scramble over the rocks,
brush past juniper branches,
to reach the top and look out
across our sunset canyon, sienna brown.

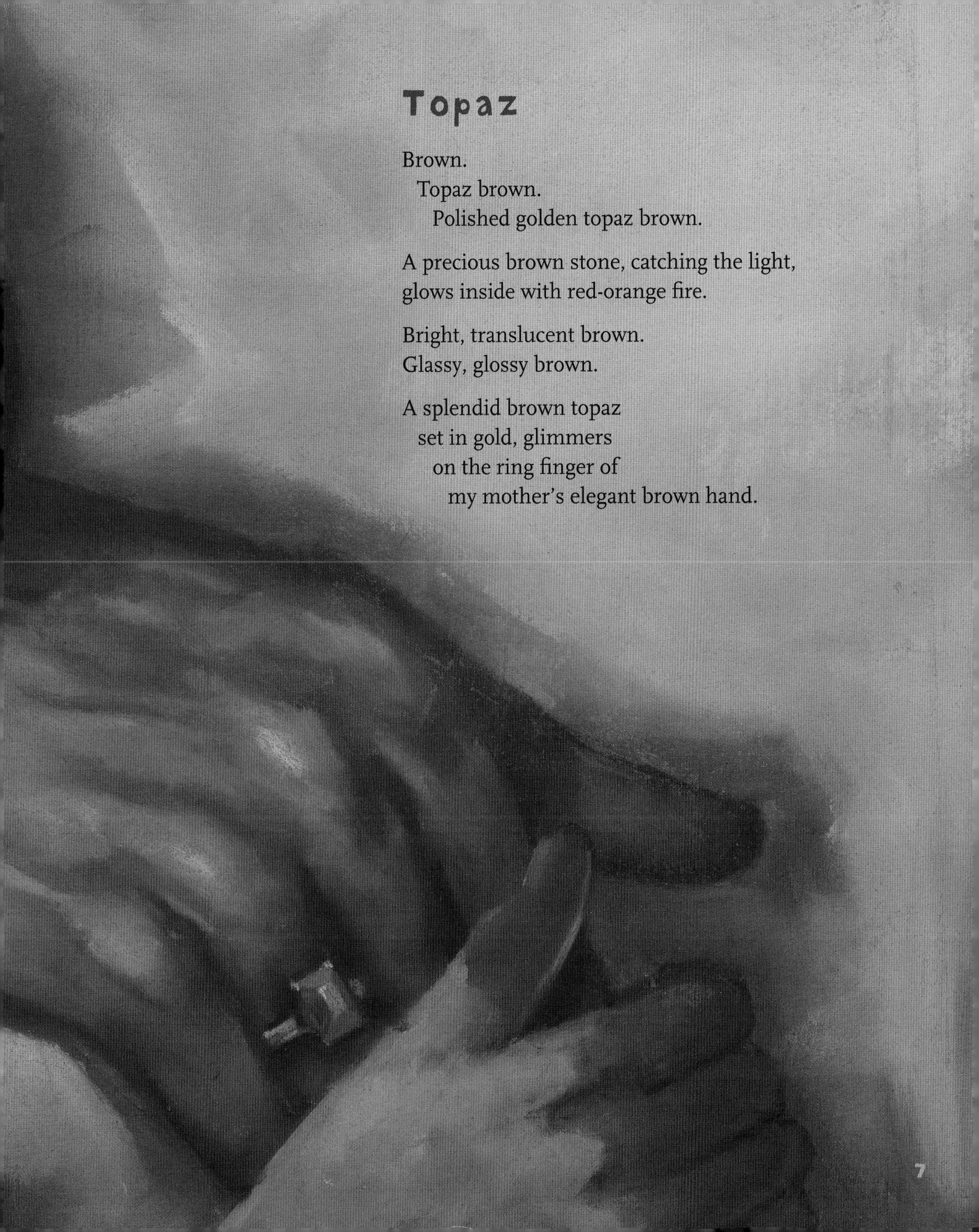

Topaz

Brown.
Topaz brown.
Polished golden topaz brown.

A precious brown stone, catching the light,
glows inside with red-orange fire.

Bright, translucent brown.
Glassy, glossy brown.

A splendid brown topaz
set in gold, glimmers
on the ring finger of
my mother's elegant brown hand.

Bay

Brown.
Russet brown.
Autumn bay-brown.

Brown leaves crunch and
crackle under our shoes in fall.

Acorns in October,
maples make red stars.

Brown to keep you warm
on cold November nights.

Snug, cozy brown.
Crisp, keen-eyed brown.

We stomp through autumn bay-brown,
kicking up leaves that tumble down,
swirl back up, and dance away
before our bay-brown eyes.

Sepia

Brown.
  Sepia brown.
    Inky, crinkly sepia brown.

Aunty's brown hand
trembles with age
but her voice rings with laughter: *Look!*
A photo from when I was young.

Wistful, muted brown.
Soft, nostalgic brown.

Is that really you, Aunty?
I see a girl with *my* face!

Look closer.
Aunty holds the photo up
next to her crinkled cheek.

The eyes! I realize.
The girl has Aunty's eyes,
  soft and shining,
    sepia brown.

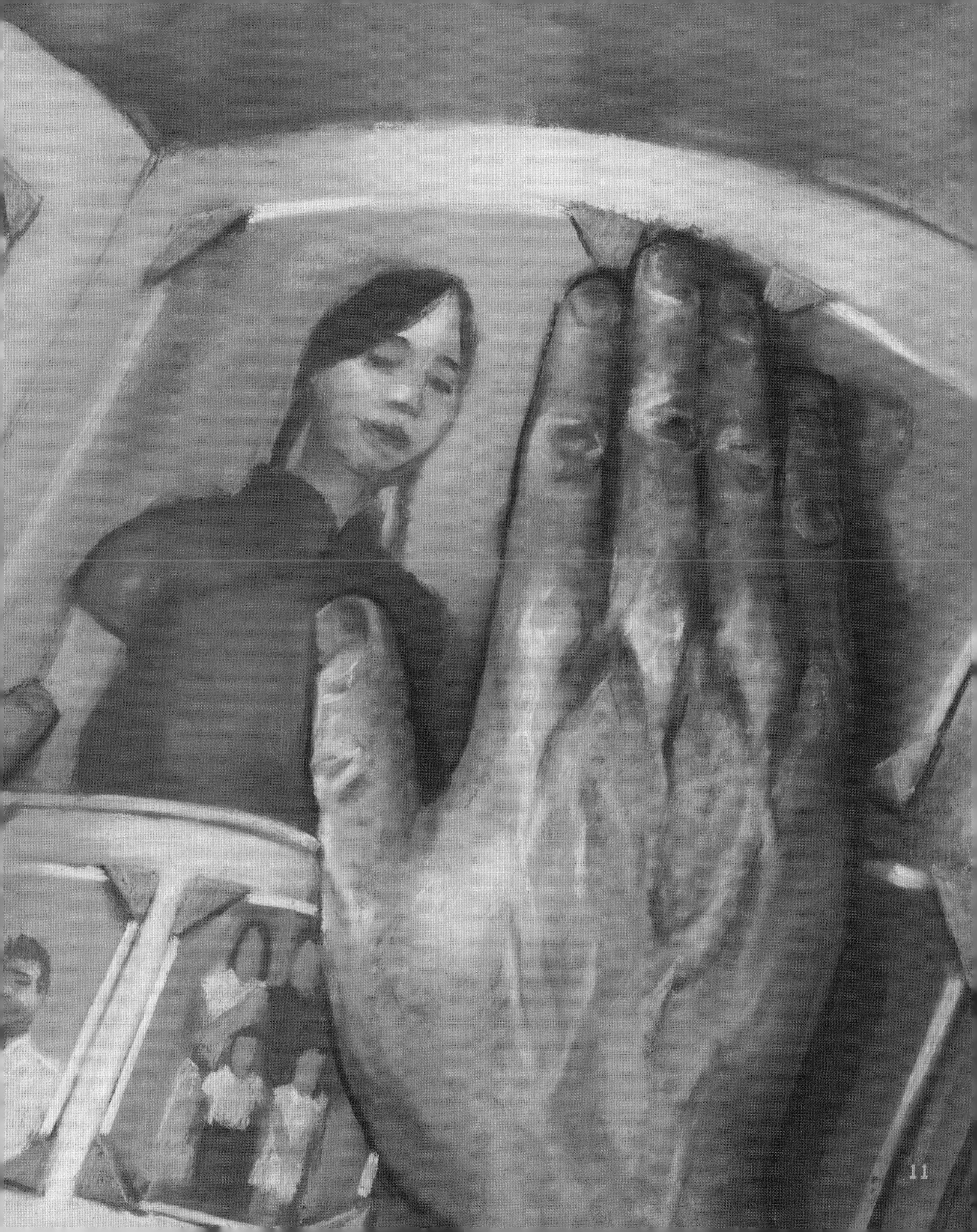

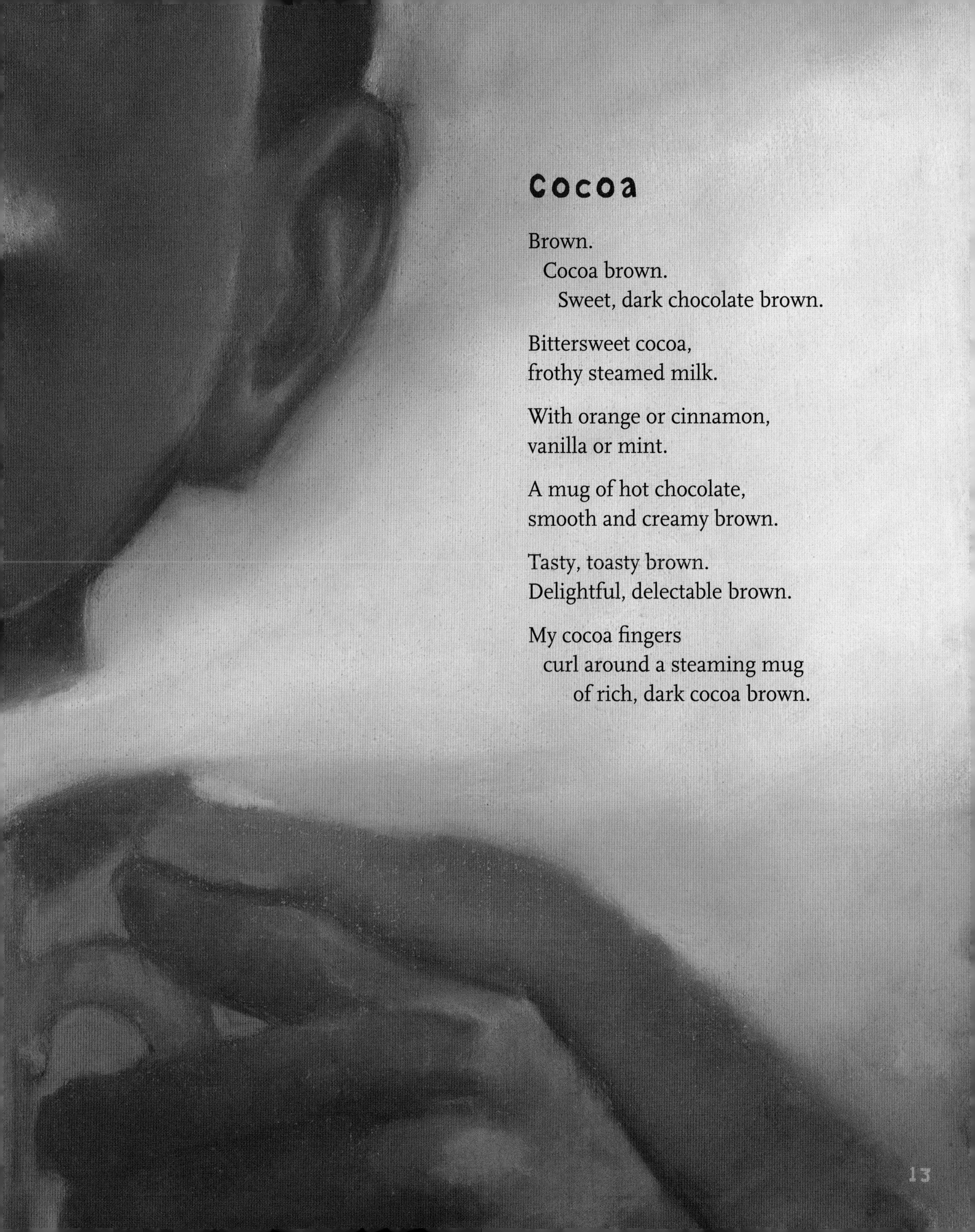

Cocoa

Brown.
Cocoa brown.
Sweet, dark chocolate brown.

Bittersweet cocoa,
frothy steamed milk.

With orange or cinnamon,
vanilla or mint.

A mug of hot chocolate,
smooth and creamy brown.

Tasty, toasty brown.
Delightful, delectable brown.

My cocoa fingers
curl around a steaming mug
of rich, dark cocoa brown.

Ocher

Brown.
  Ocher brown.
    Vivid orange-brown.

Like *mehendi* designs
on a bride's hands.

Ocher flowers, umber stems,
swirls and curls of bright orange-brown.

Joyful, festive brown.
Ornate, alluring brown.

Designs and patterns
  wind around our slim brown wrists,
    flare out like fans across our feet,
      as we dance at a wedding, celebrating
        in radiant swirls of ocher brown.

Beige

Brown.
  Beige brown.
    Warm and scratchy, sandy brown.

Seashells and sand castles,
starfish on the beach.

Rough, textured brown.
Warm-in-the-sun brown.

Bits of mica wink at us
  like shining hazel eyes
    as our feet mark out braided paths
      along the seashore, sandy brown.

Sandalwood

Brown.
  Sandalwood brown.
    Musky-scented sandalwood brown.

Ajji's sandalwood jewelry box
holds her golden bangles,
the earrings that belonged to her own Ajji.
Every ornament knows a story.

Balmy, sweet-smelling brown.
Spicy, incense-wafting brown.

Beti, Ajji tells me, *when you're grown up,*
all these things will be for you.
A hint of sandalwood scent
  clings to her sari,
    hovers around her hands,
      velvety-soft and
        sandalwood brown.

Coffee

Brown.
  Coffee brown.
    Aromatic espresso brown.

Mami in the afternoon quiet,
stirring her *café con leche*.

She mixes a little coffee
with a whole lot of milk and sugar —
that's for me.

Brisk, energizing brown.
Inviting, invigorating brown.

As I sip I think
  of the brown hands that planted,
    the brown hands that harvested,
      the brown hands that ground the beans
        to make this special drink for my
          cinnamon lips to smile over.

Adobe

Brown.
  Adobe brown.
    Rosy, warm adobe brown.

Rose-colored desert, sandstone mesa:
our adobe home rises out of the rock.
Spiky yucca plants guard our door.

Windswept desert brown.
Sheltering adobe brown.

Grandmother soaks the yucca leaves in water –
a soothing medicine for my cuts and scrapes.
Her strong, adobe hands
  look like the desert rocks,
    but her fingertips are
      soft as chamomile flowers.

Tamarind

Brown.
Tamarind brown.
Deep purplish-blackish brown.

Like the tamarind paste Amma uses
to make *chatambd, sambar,* or
spicy-tangy tamarind rice.

Crackling brown mustard seeds,
hot red pepper, curry leaves.

Add powdered spices
and blackish-brown tamarind paste.

Hot, tangy brown.
Rich, savory brown.

Spicy as supper in Madras,
tasty as lunchtime in Mumbai,
where a mother serves piping-hot *sambar*
to a daughter with two long,
tamarind-colored braids.

Spruce

Brown.
  Spruce brown.
    Rich, melodic spruce brown.

Violin, guitar and bass
built of spruce wood, burnished brown.
A honey-colored melody
drifts along our narrow street.

Humming, strumming brown.
Ringing, singing brown.

Abuelito's precise brown fingertips
move along the violin's strings.

Papá's guitar travels
through a maze of shifting chords.

Tío winks at me from behind the *contrabajo*
  as my hands clap out a staccato pattern:
    taka taka tak,
      rapid spruce brown.

Nutmeg

Brown.
  Nutmeg brown.
    Sharp, redolent nutmeg brown.

Nutmeg for gingerbread,
allspice for cider:
Grandma's treats for my cousins and me.

Fresh, musky brown.
Sweet, balmy brown.

Brown legs race to the kitchen,
  brown arms clamor around the table,
    and all our eager brown fingers
      reach for the fresh-baked treats,
        spiced with rich nutmeg brown.

Brown

Brown.
My face.
Milk-tea brown.

I am brown. I am beautiful.

Brown.
Your face.
Sienna brown
or cocoa brown,
café con leche brown or
radiant ocher brown.

Our hands, our fingers.
Cinnamon brown
or rich coffee brown,
sandalwood brown or
rosy adobe brown.

Our ankles, our feet.
Nutmeg brown
or mocha brown,
dark chocolate brown
or tawny golden brown.

Our eyes.
Luminous topaz brown
or sweet cappuccino brown,
shiny sepia brown
or twinkling hazel brown.

Our hair.
Spruce brown
or bay brown,
russet brown or
deep tamarind brown.

We are brown. We are **beautiful**.

When I was a little girl in North Carolina, I hated waiting for the school bus. Every day at the bus stop a group of older kids would call me names and make fun of my brown skin, saying brown was a dirty, ugly color. I longed to trade in my brown complexion for peachy-pink. I still remember sitting in the bathtub and hoping that if I just scrubbed hard enough the brown would go away.

As I got older, though, I began discovering lots of wonderful stories and poems about the color brown, written by and about proud brown people. When I read their words, I didn't feel ugly or dirty anymore. After all, brown was the color of cocoa and hazelnuts, coffee and tea, caramel and cinnamon. A tasty color! And brown was the color of topaz, sandalwood, copper, and bronze. A valuable color! And brown was the color of autumn, forests, and mountains. A beautiful color!

Today, when I look in the mirror, I feel happy and lucky to see a brown face smiling back at me. Because, from tan to tamarind, brown is a beautiful color.

— *Malathi Michelle Iyengar*

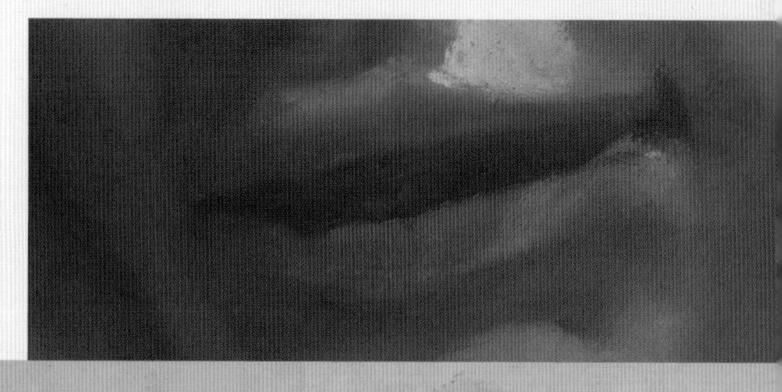

Library of Congress Cataloging-in-Publication Data
Iyengar, Malathi Michelle.
Tan to tamarind : poems about the color brown / poems by Malathi Michelle Iyengar ; illustrations by Jamel Akib.
p. cm.
ISBN 978-0-89239-227-8
1. Brown—Juvenile poetry. 2. Colors—Juvenile poetry. 3. Human skin color—Juvenile poetry. 4. Children's poetry, American. I. Akib, Jamel, ill. II. Title.
PS3609.Y46T36 2009
811'.6—dc22 2008022225

Executive Editor: Dana Goldberg Design & Art Direction: Carl Angel
Publisher & Executive Director: Lorraine García-Nakata
Thanks to the staff of Children's Book Press: Imelda Cruz, Janet del Mundo, Rod Lowe, Janine Macbeth, and Christina Troup.

Children's Book Press is a 501(c)(3) non-profit organization (FED TAX ID#94-2298885). Our work is made possible in part by the following contributors: AT&T Foundation, John Crew and Sheila Gadsden, San Francisco Foundation, San Francisco Arts Commission, Horizons Foundation, National Endowment for the Arts, Union Bank of California, Children's Book Press Board of Directors, and the Anonymous Fund of the Greater Houston Community Foundation.
For a catalog, write to: Children's Book Press, 965 Mission Street, Suite 425, San Francisco, California, 94103. Visit us on the web at: www.childrensbookpress.org

Printed in Hong Kong via Marwin Productions
10 9 8 7 6 5 4 3 2 1

Malathi Michelle Iyengar grew up in North Carolina. She holds Master's degrees in Education and in Music, and currently teaches at a public elementary school where she is happy to see lots of beautiful brown faces every day. Malathi lives in the Los Angeles area with her husband and daughter.

This book is dedicated in memory of Kumuda Iyengar. —MMI

Jamel Akib was born in England and grew up in Malaysia. His award-winning illustrations have appeared in children's books, magazines, and advertisements in the United States and abroad. He lives in England with his wife and two children.

For Jenifer, always looking over my shoulder. —JA

Distributed to the book trade by Publishers Group West.
Quantity discounts available through the publisher for nonprofit use.